BEHIND THE MULLET

UNMASKING THE DOG THE BOUNTY HUNTER

Duane Dog Chapman

WRITTEN BY:

JANE COELHO

Duane 'Dog' Chapman

ISBN: **9798883987648**

TABLE OF CONTENTS

TABLE OF CONTENTS.................................... 2

OUTLAWS AND ANGELS.............................. 7

THE TURNING POINT................................. 11

REDEMPTION IN THE HUNT...................... 14

THE RISE OF THE BOUNTY HUNTER.................. 19

THE LUSTER CASE AND INTERNATIONAL
NOTORIETY.. 23

BALANCING VIGILANTE IMAGE WITH LEGAL
BOUNDARIES.. 30

"DOG THE BOUNTY HUNTER"..................... 34

FAMILY TIES... 38

HEARTBREAK AND HEALING....................... 42

LEGAL BATTLES AND PUBLIC IMAGE
THROUGHOUT HIS CAREER......................... 46

ACCUSATIONS OF RACISM AND ADDRESSING HIS
PAST.. 51

ACTS OF GENEROSITY AND COMMUNITY WORK. 54

THE MAN BEHIND THE DOG......................... 58

THE FUTURE OF THE BOUNTY HUNTER................ 61

BORN INTO A CROSSROADS

Duane "Dog" Chapman's story begins in the foothills of the Rocky Mountains, a place of stark beauty that would come to be overshadowed by the turbulence of his youth. Born in Denver, Colorado in 1951, Duane was the product of a complex family history. His father, Wesley Duane Chapman Sr., was a butcher by trade, a man described as hardworking but prone to a restless spirit. Wesley Sr.'s own heritage was a mix of Cherokee and German, a lineage that instilled in Duane a certain toughness and a deep connection to the American West.

Duane's mother, Barbara Darlene Smith, came from a different world. A homemaker of Irish and Scottish descent, she yearned for stability, a stark contrast to Wesley Sr.'s wanderlust. This fundamental difference would soon become a fault line in their young marriage.

By 1953, when Duane was just two years old, the cracks began to show. Wesley Sr. packed his bags, leaving Barbara to raise Duane and his younger brother, Wesley Duane Jr., alone. The financial strain was immense, forcing Barbara to move her young family into a series of modest apartments and budget motels.

The instability of Duane's early life was compounded by his mother's struggles. Barbara, overwhelmed by the pressures of single parenthood, turned to alcohol as a coping mechanism. This left Duane and his brother largely unsupervised, free to roam the often-rough streets of Denver.

It was during these unsupervised years, from the mid-1950s to the early 1960s, that Duane's brushes with the law began. Petty theft, vandalism, and running away from home became a troubling pattern. He gravitated towards other troubled youngsters, forming a loose-knit group that reveled in pushing boundaries and testing their luck.

By his mid-teens, Duane's defiance escalated. In 1967, at the age of 16, he was arrested for the first time, a wake-up call that did little to deter him. The allure of life on the edge, the thrill of defying authority, proved too strong.

Throughout this period, Duane's relationship with his father remained distant. Wesley Sr. would occasionally reappear, offering empty promises and fleeting moments of connection, before disappearing once again. This emotional inconsistency left a deep scar on Duane, fostering a sense of abandonment and a yearning for a strong male role model, a yearning that would shape his future choices in unexpected ways.

By 1976, at the age of 25, Duane Chapman had become a familiar face in Denver's petty crime scene. His life was a chaotic mix of adrenaline-fueled escapades and brushes with the authorities. It was a path that would lead him far from the foothills of Colorado, to a life defined by chasing fugitives and confronting the darkness that lurked within himself.

OUTLAWS AND ANGELS

By 1967, the cracks in Duane Chapman's life had become canyons. At 16, his brushes with the law had escalated from petty theft to more serious offenses. The instability of his childhood, coupled with his absent father and his mother's struggles, had left him adrift, searching for a sense of belonging. It was in this emotional maelstrom that Duane found himself drawn to the alluring rumble of motorcycles and the perceived camaraderie of outlaw motorcycle clubs.

The year was 1968, and the Devils Diciples, a notorious motorcycle club with a reputation for violence and rebellion, held a dark magnetism for the young Duane. Founded in California in the 1960s, the Devils Diciples embodied a counter-culture lifestyle that resonated with Duane's yearning for acceptance and a sense of belonging. He saw in them a brotherhood, a group of men who lived by their own rules, defying societal norms and carving their own path.

Joining the Devils Diciples at the tender age of 17 was a pivotal moment for Duane. He embraced the club's outlaw culture, the thrill of motorcycle rallies, and the sense of purpose that came with being part of a tightly knit group. However, this newfound sense of belonging came at a cost. The club's criminal activities, often involving drug dealing and violence, placed Duane further down a dangerous path.

While the exact details remain murky, it was around this time, in 1971, that Duane met LaFonda Boone, a young woman who would become his first wife. LaFonda, with her dreams and aspirations, offered a glimpse of stability amidst the chaos of Duane's life. Despite the allure of a normal life, the weight of his loyalty to the club and the adrenaline-fueled lifestyle he had grown accustomed to proved too strong. Blinded by this misplaced sense of belonging, Duane chose the outlaws over building a future with LaFonda.

In 1976, a fateful event would shatter the fragile world Duane had built. While on a club errand, a drug deal gone wrong escalated into violence. Duane, according to court records, was waiting in a getaway car while a friend, Donald Wayne Kuykendall, entered a house to buy marijuana. A struggle ensued, and Kuykendall fatally shot the homeowner. Duane, though not directly involved in the shooting, was charged with first-degree murder as an accomplice.

This incident marked a turning point in Duane's life. Facing a lengthy prison sentence, his fledgling marriage with LaFonda crumbled under the weight of the impending legal battle. LaFonda, unable to handle the uncertainty and the dark cloud hanging over their future, divorced Duane and married his best friend, a devastating blow that added to the emotional turmoil he was already experiencing.

Sentenced to five years in prison, Duane entered the Texas State Penitentiary in Huntsville, Texas, in 1976. The roar of motorcycles and the camaraderie of the club were replaced by the clanging of cell doors and the harsh realities of prison life. It was within these stark walls that Duane would begin a long and arduous journey of self-discovery, a journey that would ultimately lead him away from the world of outlaws and towards a life defined by chasing fugitives.

THE TURNING POINT

The year 1976 marked a seismic shift in the life of Duane "Dog" Chapman. Just 25 years old, the brash, rebellious youth found himself facing the stark reality of a prison cell. This dramatic turn of events stemmed from a fateful incident that shattered his world and forced him to confront the consequences of his choices.

It all began with a drug deal gone tragically wrong. Duane, a member of the notorious Devils Diciples motorcycle club, was entangled in a violent crime. While details remain murky, court records paint a grim picture. In 1976, while waiting in a getaway car during a marijuana purchase, Duane's friend, Donald Wayne Kuykendall, became embroiled in a struggle with the homeowner that resulted in the homeowner's death. Though not directly involved in the shooting, Duane was charged with first-degree murder as an accomplice – a harsh reality that would change the course of his life.

11

The weight of the impending legal battle proved too much for Duane's fledgling marriage. LaFonda Boone, his wife of a few short years, crumbled under the pressure. Unable to face the uncertainty and the stigma attached to Duane's situation, she filed for divorce, a devastating blow that added to his emotional turmoil.

The verdict was a hammer blow. Found guilty, Duane was sentenced to five years in the Texas State Penitentiary in Huntsville, Texas. The roar of motorcycles and the camaraderie of the club were replaced by the deafening silence of a prison cell and the harsh realities of incarceration. Gone were the days of reckless abandon and misplaced loyalty. In their place, a cold, hard reality set in.

Within the stark confines of the prison walls, Duane's life underwent a profound transformation. The carefree young man, hardened by a turbulent childhood and drawn to the outlaw life, began a long and arduous journey of self-discovery. He wrestled with guilt, regret, and the consequences of his actions.

It was during this period of introspection that Duane encountered a pivotal moment. Witnessing a brutal prison fight, he experienced a profound conversion. He vowed to turn his life around, to use his strength and street smarts for good instead of causing further harm. This newfound resolve became the seed from which his future career in bounty hunting would blossom.

Duane's time in prison was a turning point, a brutal crucible that forged a new path. He emerged from those walls a changed man, one determined to atone for his past and embrace a life dedicated to pursuing justice. The impulsive youth, fueled by rebellion, was slowly giving way to the resolute figure who would become synonymous with the name "Dog the Bounty Hunter."

REDEMPTION IN THE HUNT

The year 1976 was a pivotal one for Duane Chapman. Walking through the gates of the Texas State Penitentiary as a convicted felon, he emerged five years later a changed man. The impulsive youth, hardened by a turbulent childhood and drawn to the outlaw life, had been replaced by a man determined to forge a new path. Fueled by a newfound resolve and a desire for redemption, Duane embarked on a journey that would not only redefine his life but also propel him into the national spotlight.

Duane's initial foray into the world outside prison walls was far from glamorous. Released in 1980, he found himself navigating a challenging economic landscape. Job opportunities for an ex-convict were scarce, forcing him to take on any work he could find. It was during this time, through a series of manual labor jobs, that Duane encountered the world of bail bonds.

The bail bond industry, a complex system where individuals or companies provide financial guarantees to secure the release of defendants awaiting trial, intrigued Duane. He saw in it an opportunity to utilize his street smarts and his newfound commitment to justice. Determined to learn the ropes, he landed a job as a bondsman with Weldon Lacy, a local bail bondsman in Colorado.

Working alongside Lacy proved to be a turning point. Duane, a quick learner with a natural charisma, excelled in the role. He honed his skills in tracking down fugitives who had skipped bail, a task that required resourcefulness, persistence, and a keen understanding of human behavior. This period also marked the birth of his now-iconic persona, "Dog." The name, a reflection of his relentless pursuit and unwavering determination, resonated with both colleagues and fugitives alike.

However, Duane's ambition extended beyond being a skilled bondsman. He envisioned building his own bail bond company, a place where he could not only utilize his talents but also create a team dedicated to upholding the law. This dream, however, was not without its challenges. Securing funding and navigating the legal hurdles associated with starting a bail bond business proved to be a daunting task for a former convict.

Despite the odds stacked against him, Duane persevered. Drawing strength from his unwavering determination and his growing reputation as a skilled bounty hunter, he secured the necessary licenses and funding in the early 1980s. Thus, "Dog the Bounty Hunter" officially became a force to be reckoned with, with the establishment of his own bail bond company.

Building a successful business from the ground up was no easy feat. Duane, however, was not one to shy away from hard work. He recruited a team of individuals who shared his commitment to justice and his relentless work ethic. Together, they tackled even the most challenging cases, establishing a reputation for efficiency and effectiveness.

Balancing his burgeoning business with his personal life also presented a set of challenges. In 1979, while still on parole, Duane met Beth Smith, a woman who would become his anchor and his partner in crime-fighting (quite literally). Beth, a strong and independent woman, not only brought stability to Duane's life but also became an integral part of his business. Their partnership, both personal and professional, blossomed in the early 1980s as they navigated the complex world of bail bonds and bounty hunting together.

By the mid-1980s, Duane "Dog" Chapman had successfully transitioned from a troubled youth to a respected figure in the bail bond industry. His company was thriving, and his reputation as a tenacious bounty hunter preceded him. Little did he know, however, that a chance encounter in the

Duane 'Dog' Chapman

late 1980s would propel him and his
unconventional methods of pursuing justice into
the national spotlight, forever changing the course
of his life.

THE RISE OF THE BOUNTY HUNTER

The mid-1980s saw Duane "Dog" Chapman firmly established in the world of bail bonds. His tenacity, honed during his time as a bounty hunter for Weldon Lacy, coupled with his newly formed company, had earned him a reputation for efficiency and an almost mythical ability to track down fugitives. However, it was a series of high-profile captures in the late 1980s that would catapult him from a respected bail bondsman to a national icon.

One such capture, etched in the annals of bounty hunting lore, involved Max Factor heir Andrew Luster. In 1989, Luster, accused of multiple counts of rape, fled bail in California. Dog, ever the relentless pursuer, tracked him down in Puerto Vallarta, Mexico. This daring capture, which involved navigating a foreign legal system and overcoming logistical hurdles, not only brought Luster to justice but also garnered Dog significant media attention. News outlets across the nation were captivated by his unconventional tactics and his unwavering determination.

The Luster case was a tipping point. Dog's success, along with his charismatic personality and no-nonsense approach, resonated with the public. He became a symbol of a justice system that, for some, felt sluggish and impersonal. Dog, with his booming voice, his ever-present bandanna, and his team of loyal operatives, offered a sense of finality — a guarantee that fugitives would be apprehended, no matter the cost.

This newfound fame, however, was a double-edged sword. While Dog's reputation as a skilled bounty hunter soared, his methods also attracted scrutiny. Critics questioned his aggressive tactics, accusing him of operating outside the bounds of the law. Legal battles ensued, with some questioning the legality of his cross-border pursuits. Dog, however, remained undeterred. He believed in his methods and his unwavering commitment to bringing fugitives to justice.

Throughout the early 1990s, Dog continued to make headlines with a series of high-profile captures. Each successful apprehension, each daring chase, further solidified his image as a modern-day bounty hunter. He became a controversial figure, admired by some for his dedication and criticized by others for his methods.

Love him or hate him, there was no denying Dog Chapman's impact. He had not only established himself as a force to be reckoned with in the bail bond industry but had also redefined the public perception of bounty hunting. His rise to fame, however, was just the beginning. Little did he know, a chance encounter in Hawaii in the late 1990s would lead to an even greater platform, a reality television show that would propel him and his family into the living rooms of millions across the globe.

Duane 'Dog' Chapman

THE LUSTER CASE AND INTERNATIONAL NOTORIETY

The year was 2003. California was abuzz with a story that sent shivers down spines. Andrew Luster, the handsome heir to the Max Factor cosmetics empire, a name synonymous with beauty and glamour, stood accused of horrific crimes. The charges were numerous – 86 counts in total – each a sickening testament to a dark side lurking beneath the veneer of wealth and privilege. Luster was alleged to have drugged and raped multiple women, a betrayal that shattered their sense of security and left a trail of trauma in its wake.

As the trial progressed, a sense of unease began to grow. Luster, facing a daunting possibility of a lengthy prison sentence, vanished without a trace. This wasn't a dramatic escape orchestrated for the movies; it was a calculated move, a desperate attempt to outrun justice. He became a fugitive, a wealthy ghost flitting across international borders, leaving the Californian justice system grappling with his absence.

Meanwhile, across the country, Duane "Dog" Chapman, a household name synonymous with his own brand of justice, watched the news unfold. Chapman, a former bail bondsman, had carved a niche for himself in the world of reality television with his show "Dog the Bounty Hunter." He was a gruff, unconventional figure, known for his unwavering commitment to bringing criminals to justice, often operating in the fringes of the legal system.

The Luster case resonated deeply with Chapman. Here was a predator, a man who used his wealth and status as a weapon, preying on the vulnerable. For Chapman, it was a personal crusade, a chance to ensure a dangerous man wouldn't disappear into the shadows. Fueled by this sense of purpose, Chapman and his team, including his son Leland

and longtime associate Tim Chapman, embarked on a relentless pursuit.

Their investigation led them to Puerto Vallarta, Mexico, a sun-drenched paradise that had become a haven for fugitives seeking escape. For months, the Chapmans blended in, living under assumed identities, their days filled with the constant vigilance of the hunt. Finally, on June 18, 2003, their patience paid off. In a scene ripped from a crime thriller, they apprehended Luster.

The capture, however, was far from straightforward. Mexican authorities, alerted by the commotion, intervened, arresting all four men – the fugitive and his captors. The situation became a tangled web of legalities. Bounty hunting, a mainstay of Chapman's business in the U.S., was illegal in Mexico. While Luster was quickly extradited back to California to face his 125-year sentence, the Chapmans found themselves facing a new set of charges – "deprivation of liberty" – a legal concept with significant implications.

Initially denied bail, the Chapmans experienced the harsh realities of a foreign prison system. But Beth Chapman, Dog's wife and a formidable force in her own right, rallied public opinion back in the U.S. With media attention mounting, they were eventually granted bail. However, against their lawyer's advice, they made a risky decision – they fled Mexico, becoming international fugitives themselves.

The following years were a period of constant uncertainty. In September 2006, U.S. Marshals arrested the Chapmans in Hawaii, acting on behalf of the Mexican government. The legal battle that ensued was a complex dance. Chapman's defense argued that the Mexican charges, misdemeanors in their own right, amounted to felony kidnapping under American law. The Mexican authorities countered this claim, insisting on Luster's illegal capture.

The case became a political spectacle. U.S. Congressmen weighed in, pressuring the State Department to block extradition. Chapman himself took to the media, portraying himself as a victim of a corrupt system, a narrative that resonated with some viewers. The legal proceedings in Mexico crawled at a glacial pace, hearings postponed, and new evidence demanded.

A glimmer of hope emerged in August 2007 when a Mexican court ruled that the statute of limitations on the Chapmans' arrest had likely expired. This potentially invalidated the warrants against them. Finally, in August of that same year, the First Criminal Court in Puerto Vallarta dismissed all charges. The prosecution appealed, as is standard practice in Mexico, but the Chapmans' long ordeal seemed to be nearing its end. On November 5, 2007, a U.S. Magistrate Judge made the final call, dismissing Mexico's extradition request. News of the decision was met with both relief and criticism.

The capture of Andrew Luster and the subsequent legal battle involving Duane "Dog" Chapman remain a controversial and complex chapter in legal history. The lines between justice and vigilantism blurred. Chapman, painted by some as a hero who brought a dangerous predator to face his accusers, was simultaneously condemned by others for his disregard of international law.

Luster's crimes were reprehensible, and his conviction served as a measure of justice for his victims. Yet, questions linger about the legality of Chapman's actions. His decision to track down a convicted felon across borders raises ethical dilemmas about the limits of bounty hunting and the complex interplay between legal systems in different countries.

The case also highlights the power of media and public opinion in shaping legal narratives. Chapman's relentless media campaign undoubtedly influenced his eventual victory against extradition. And while the spotlight shines brightly on Chapman and Luster, it's important to remember the true victims of this story: the women Luster assaulted, whose trauma and fight for justice will continue long after the headlines fade.

The story of Andrew Luster and Duane "Dog" Chapman, is thus one of blurred lines, moral quandaries, and consequences that ripple through time. Its legacy continues to be debated in discussions about justice, the role of bounty hunters, and the often-uneasy relationship between the United States and Mexico.

BALANCING VIGILANTE IMAGE WITH LEGAL BOUNDARIES

Duane "Dog" Chapman, the name that became synonymous with relentless pursuit and unwavering justice, rose to prominence in the late 1980s. His success in capturing fugitives, particularly the high-profile case of Andrew Luster, propelled him into the national spotlight. However, with this newfound fame came intense scrutiny. Dog, a man who thrived on action and results, found himself constantly walking a tightrope between his vigilante image and the boundaries of the legal system.

Dog's methods, characterized by bold tactics and a willingness to push the limits, resonated with a segment of the public who felt the traditional justice system was slow and impersonal. They saw him as a symbol of swift and uncompromising justice, a man who delivered fugitives to the authorities no matter the cost.

However, critics viewed these same tactics with a wary eye. His aggressive pursuits, often conducted across state lines and even into foreign territories, raised questions about legality and due process. Legal battles ensued, with some challenging the validity of his captures, particularly those outside the United States. Dog, ever the fighter, remained undeterred. He firmly believed in his methods and his unwavering commitment to bringing fugitives to justice.

Throughout the late 1980s and early 1990s, Dog continued to operate in this gray area. Each successful capture, each daring chase, further solidified his image as a modern-day bounty hunter, blurring the lines between reality and the romanticized image portrayed in popular culture.

Dog understood the power of this image. He cultivated his persona, the ever-present bandana, the booming voice, and the loyal team of operatives by his side. This larger-than-life persona, while captivating audiences, also served a strategic purpose. It deflected attention from the complexities of his work and the legal tightrope he constantly walked.

Dog's approach to bounty hunting was undeniably effective. His success rate was impressive, and he brought numerous fugitives to justice. However, the legal battles and public scrutiny took a toll. He faced lawsuits, accusations of excessive force, and even potential criminal charges.

This period forced Dog to navigate a delicate balance. He needed to maintain his effectiveness as a bounty hunter while adhering to the legal boundaries that often felt restrictive. He began working more closely with law enforcement, collaborating on cases and ensuring his captures were conducted within the framework of the law.

The late 1980s and early 2000s were a period of both triumph and tribulation for Dog Chapman. He became a household name, a symbol of both admiration and controversy. This period also marked his evolution – from a skilled bounty hunter operating on the fringes to a figure who, while retaining his core principles, recognized the importance of operating within the legal system. This evolution would pave the way for the next chapter in his life – a reality television show that would showcase his work and the complexities of pursuing justice to a global audience.

Duane 'Dog' Chapman

"DOG THE BOUNTY HUNTER"

By the early 2000s, Duane "Dog" Chapman was a force with which to be reckoned in the world of bounty hunting. With a series of high-profile captures and a reputation for relentless pursuit, he had become a national sensation. Then came a fateful encounter that would change the trajectory of his life forever – a documentary crew who saw the potential for a captivating reality television show.

The series, ultimately titled "Dog the Bounty Hunter," premiered in 2003 on A&E. The premise was simple yet irresistible: viewers were offered an inside look at the chaotic and often dangerous world of pursuing fugitives. Dog, with his larger-than-life personality, his unconventional tactics, and a loyal team of family and friends, provided the perfect combination of drama, action, and heart.

The show quickly became a ratings juggernaut. Audiences were captivated by the adrenaline-fueled chases, the emotional complexities of capturing fugitives, and the often-dysfunctional dynamics of the Chapman family. Dog's charisma, Beth Chapman's no-nonsense attitude, and the rollercoaster of their personal and professional lives created a compelling narrative that resonated with viewers worldwide.

While the show propelled Dog to stratospheric levels of fame, it also came with a significant price. His life, once lived in relative anonymity, was now constantly under the public microscope. The distinction between "Dog the Bounty Hunter" and Duane, the father, husband, and deeply spiritual man, started to blur. Maintaining privacy with a camera crew following his every move became near impossible.

The show also brought increased scrutiny and amplified the criticism surrounding Dog's methods.

Some accused producers of exaggerating certain aspects of bounty hunting for dramatic effect, while others questioned the ethical implications of showcasing the lives of fugitives and their families for entertainment purposes.

Despite the controversies, "Dog the Bounty Hunter" ran for eight successful seasons, solidifying Dog's status as a pop culture icon. It showcased the behind-the-scenes workings of bail bonds and bounty hunting, offering audiences a glimpse into the complex and often misunderstood world of pursuing justice outside traditional law enforcement channels.

The show humanized Dog, revealing his vulnerabilities along with his unwavering dedication. Viewers witnessed the emotional toll of his work, the complex relationships within his family, and his moments of self-doubt. This raw and often unfiltered portrayal added a layer of depth to the larger-than-life persona carefully crafted for the cameras.

"Dog the Bounty Hunter" transformed not only Dog's career but his entire life. He became a global brand, expanding into merchandise, books, and even speaking engagements. However, the constant spotlight led to personal struggles, straining relationships and exposing both his flaws and his triumphs for the world to see.

The legacy of "Dog the Bounty Hunter" is undeniable. It redefined the reality television genre, showcasing a gritty reality far removed from the often-scripted narratives of other popular shows. It also sparked important conversations about the role of bounty hunters within the justice system, highlighting the complexities and controversies surrounding the profession. Dog, the man at the center of it all, had gone from a convict to a television icon.

FAMILY TIES

Behind the leather, bandanas, and the unwavering pursuit of fugitives, Duane "Dog" Chapman's personal life was a complex and often turbulent tapestry of familial bonds, love, and loss. His family ties formed a core part of his being, influencing his journey and often shaping the public narrative surrounding him.

Duane's journey as a father began early. Over the course of his life, he became both biological and adoptive father to twelve children. From his early and short-lived marriages to LaFonda and Ann Tegnell, came sons Duane Lee II, Leland, Zebediah, and Wesley. His third marriage, to Lyssa Rae Brittain, brought daughters Barbara Katie, Lyssa "Baby Lyssa" Rae, and son Tucker Dee to the Chapman clan.

However, his relationships with his children were anything but idyllic. Marked by his early life's turbulence, his time in prison, and his demanding career, their connections were often strained and filled with complexities. Some of his sons, namely Duane Lee II and Leland, joined him in the bounty hunting business adding a unique layer to their father-son bonds. Yet, even those professional collaborations were far from simple. Duane's demanding personality clashed with his sons' desires for independence and recognition for their contributions, resulting in frequent friction and fallouts.

Duane's multiple marriages created a large, blended family – a testament to his tumultuous love life and his attempts to find stability. His unions, spanning from the 1970s to 2006, were often short-lived and volatile, ending in painful divorces and battles for custody. The result was a family unit where children were tied together not just by a shared last name, but also by shared experiences of trauma, hardship, and a life in the relentless public eye.

However, one relationship stood out as a beacon of both strength and complexity: his partnership with Beth Smith. Duane met Beth in 1979, a tumultuous time when he was on parole and navigating life after prison. Beth, a fiery and independent woman, became his rock, his confidante, and his unwavering partner in both life and in the pursuit of fugitives. Their marriage, officially formalized years later in 2006, was a whirlwind of passion, conflict, and a profound devotion that transcended their explosive personalities.

Beth brought a new dimension to Dog's life. She challenged him, softened his rough edges, and became an integral part of both his personal evolution and his professional success. Their bond was undeniable, a force to be reckoned with. Their televised arguments and raw displays of love and dysfunction captivated viewers of "Dog the Bounty Hunter," offering a glimpse into the heart of their complex marriage.

Yet, their union was also plagued by insecurities and demons from their past. Duane's tumultuous history and Beth's battle with addiction became recurring themes in their tumultuous yet captivating relationship. The cameras captured their struggles for all to see, adding a layer of vulnerability to their already captivating public image.

Duane Chapman's family life was as chaotic and captivating as the pursuits that made him famous. From his troubled relationships with his children to the dynamics of his blended families and his profound partnership with Beth, his personal life was a reflection of his own struggles, triumphs, and unwavering determination to find solace amidst the chaos. His family ties are a reminder that even the toughest bounty hunter is shaped and influenced by those he loves, and that even the most unconventional relationships can hold the power of transformative love.

HEARTBREAK AND HEALING

In 2019, tragedy struck the heart of the Chapman family and sent shockwaves through the world of "Dog the Bounty Hunter." Beth Chapman, the formidable woman who had stood by Duane's side for decades, succumbed to a long battle with cancer on June 26th. Her loss left an unfillable void in Duane's life, shattering his world and forcing him to grapple with unimaginable grief.

The months following Beth's passing were a blur of sorrow for Duane. The gruff, larger-than-life bounty hunter was unmoored, his trademark bravado masking a deep vulnerability. He struggled to find his footing; his days were consumed by an overwhelming sense of loss and a desperate yearning for the woman who had been his rock, his partner, his reason for fighting.

Grieving in the public eye added to the complexity of his pain. Fans, well-acquainted with Beth through the reality show, mourned alongside Duane. Well-wishers sent condolences, but the constant reminders of his loss amplified his anguish. The absence of Beth's fiery spirit and unwavering presence echoed through their family home and bounty hunting office, serving as a constant reminder of what had been lost.

In this period of profound grief, controversy followed Duane. Just months after Beth's passing, he began a relationship with Francie Frane, a woman who had initially reached out to offer condolences. This whirlwind romance triggered intense criticism from some fans and family members who felt he was betraying Beth's memory by moving on too quickly. Accusations of insensitivity and disrespect filled the tabloids, adding a layer of public scrutiny to Duane's already heavy burden of grief.

Despite the backlash, Duane found solace in his connection with Francie. They bonded over their shared experiences of loss – Francie had recently lost her husband – and found comfort in each other's company. Duane and Francie married in 2021, a decision that continued to stir controversy but showcased Duane's determination to find love and happiness once again.

The loss of a life partner forces a fundamental re-evaluation of priorities and a redefining of purpose. For Duane, Beth's passing and the subsequent whirlwind of grief and controversy pushed him towards a profound introspection. He wrestled with questions of legacy, the weight of mortality, and the importance of family in the grand scheme of his turbulent life.

Duane, a man defined by action, channeled some of his grief into a renewed focus on bounty hunting. He embarked on new pursuits, seeking distraction and a sense of purpose in those familiar adrenaline-fueled chases. He also found solace in leaning on his remaining children and the blended family he and Beth had built together.

While Beth's absence continues to leave a void in Duane's life and in the hearts of those who loved her, Duane has begun to forge a path forward. Balancing a deep respect for Beth and the legacy their unique bond created, he embraces his newfound love with Francie, redefining family and finding a reason to continue the chase, not just for fugitives, but for a fulfilling life in the face of immense heartbreak.

LEGAL BATTLES AND PUBLIC IMAGE THROUGHOUT HIS CAREER

Throughout his life as a bounty hunter, Duane "Dog" Chapman often walked a fine line between relentless pursuer of justice and a figure operating on the fringes of lawfulness. His audacious captures and uncompromising tactics, while applauded by some, earned him an equally fervent set of detractors. This clash of perspectives fueled numerous legal battles that punctuated his career, shaping both his public image and the very nature of bounty hunting itself.

Early in his career, Dog's methods often drew ire and resulted in lawsuits. In 1976, his involvement in a drug deal gone wrong led to convictions and prison time. While he turned his life around after parole, the specter of this incident would occasionally resurface in the form of critics questioning his suitability as a bounty hunter.

As his notoriety grew throughout the 1980s, so did the legal challenges. His daring capture of Max Factor heir Andrew Luster in 1989, though celebrated by many, resulted in accusations of kidnapping, since Luster was apprehended on Mexican soil without following proper extradition procedures. Dog, along with his team, faced charges in Mexico. Though they were later dropped due to a lack of extradition treaties, this incident set a precedent for future legal entanglements regarding cross-border pursuits.

The launch of "Dog the Bounty Hunter" in 2004 catapulted his fame to new heights, but it also amplified the scrutiny surrounding his activities. Accusations of excessive force, illegal searches, and violation of fugitives' rights became commonplace. Lawsuits from captured individuals piled up, alleging mistreatment and unlawful practices.

Some of these legal battles had significant ramifications. In 2006, a judge in Hawaii ruled that the Chapmans had violated the state's licensing requirements for bail bondsmen, leading to temporary restrictions on their work. Though he eventually regained his license, this ruling created a precedent that would inform future regulations governing bounty hunters in various states.

Dog's public image, inseparable from his profession, was a constant roller coaster. He was hailed as a hero by some for his relentless commitment to bringing fugitives to justice. Simultaneously, he was criticized for his vigilante-like approach, with detractors questioning his authority to operate outside of traditional law enforcement channels.

It's important to note that Dog's legal battles often had less to do with black-and-white lawbreaking and more with the gray areas inherent in bounty hunting. The very nature of apprehending individuals who have skipped bail involves a certain level of force and intrusion. Dog's willingness to push those boundaries to their limits often landed him in hot water with authorities and courts.

While Dog undoubtedly faced his share of legal setbacks, he was rarely deterred. He viewed these battles as a necessary part of his pursuit of justice, a testament to his unwavering belief in his methods. Despite the lawsuits and public criticism, Dog continued to operate in his characteristically bold style.

His numerous legal battles had a ripple effect across the broader landscape of bounty hunting. They helped expose the complexities of this profession and highlight the delicate balance between the rights of fugitives and the need to enforce justice. Dog Chapman's very name, whether celebrated or reviled, became synonymous with the ongoing debate about the limits of bounty hunting and its place within the modern legal system.

Duane 'Dog' Chapman

ACCUSATIONS OF RACISM AND ADDRESSING HIS PAST

Duane "Dog" Chapman's life has been a whirlwind of daring captures, public fame, and intense controversy. One recurring point of contention has been accusations of racism, a complex issue that has shadowed him throughout his career. To understand this controversy, we need to delve into specific incidents and examine how Dog has addressed his past.

In 2007, a leaked phone conversation revealed Dog using racial slurs. This incident sparked public outrage, forcing him to confront accusations of racism. Dog's defense centered around his upbringing in a racially diverse environment and his claim that the term used was a casual expression within his social circle at the time. However, many saw this as a weak explanation, highlighting the offensive nature of the language regardless of context.

Further fueling the controversy was his daughter, Bonnie Chapman's claims in 2019. She accused Dog of harboring racist views and using derogatory language towards her biracial partners. This public family feud added another layer of complexity, presenting a personal perspective that resonated with viewers questioning Dog's sincerity in addressing his past.

Dog's response to these accusations has been inconsistent. At times, he vehemently denied being racist, citing his Native American ancestry and his long history working with people of color within the bounty hunting world. However, his denials often came across as dismissive, lacking a genuine understanding of the hurtful impact of his words.

In recent years, there have been signs of a shift in Dog's approach. He has acknowledged the offensiveness of his past language and expressed a willingness to learn and grow. While some remain skeptical, this willingness to engage in difficult conversations offers a glimmer of hope for true progress.

It's crucial to examine these issues within the context of Dog's life. He grew up in a different era, a time when racial attitudes were far less sensitive than they are today. While that doesn't excuse his past behavior, it underscores the importance of personal growth and evolution.

Dog's story serves as a reminder of the ongoing struggle for racial justice. It highlights the power of personal narratives in exposing past prejudices and the importance of open dialogue in fostering understanding. Whether Dog can truly move beyond his past remains to be seen. However, his willingness to acknowledge his mistakes and engage in reflection offers a path towards reconciliation and positive change.

ACTS OF GENEROSITY AND COMMUNITY WORK

Duane "Dog" Chapman, a name synonymous with relentless pursuit and captivating television, has a reputation that often overshadows his acts of generosity and community work. While controversies and legal battles have dominated headlines, a lesser-known side of Dog reveals a man committed to giving back and supporting those in need.

Dog's acts of generosity often stem from his personal experiences. Having faced hardship and incarceration himself, he understands the importance of second chances and a helping hand. One notable example of his compassion came in 2008, when he established the "Dog's Unleashed Bail Bonds Scholarship." This scholarship aimed to offer financial assistance to students pursuing criminal justice degrees. Dog recognized the challenges faced by aspiring law enforcement professionals and believed in fostering a new generation dedicated to upholding the law.

Beyond financial aid, Dog has also dedicated time and resources to youth outreach programs. He understands the importance of steering young people away from a life of crime and violence. Through mentorship initiatives and motivational speaking engagements, he shares his own story, highlighting the pitfalls of his past and the value of making positive choices. His direct, no-nonsense approach resonates with some young people, offering a stark reality check and a path towards a more fulfilling life.

Dog's generosity extends beyond the criminal justice realm. He has participated in numerous charitable endeavors, lending his name and star power to raise awareness for various causes. From supporting cancer research in memory of his late wife, Beth, to assisting families affected by natural disasters, Dog has shown a willingness to use his platform for positive change.

However, Dog's charitable efforts are not without their complexities. His past legal troubles and controversial persona sometimes overshadow his good deeds. Critics view his philanthropic endeavors as mere attempts to improve his public image. Whether motivated by a genuine desire to help or a calculated public relations strategy, the impact remains the same: individuals and communities benefit from his generosity.

Looking beyond the motives, Dog's acts of compassion highlight a multifaceted individual. He is not just the larger-than-life bounty hunter portrayed on television. He is a man who understands the importance of giving back, of offering support to those struggling, and of fostering positive change within the communities he touches.

Duane 'Dog' Chapman

While Dog Chapman's life story is riddled with controversy, his acts of generosity paint a more nuanced picture. He is a man shaped by both his past struggles and his desire to make a positive impact on the world. His commitment to supporting students, mentoring youth, and contributing to worthy causes deserves recognition, reminding us that even the most complex figures can possess a capacity for compassion and generosity.

THE MAN BEHIND THE DOG

Duane "Dog" Chapman, the name that elicits images of steely determination, booming commands, and a relentless pursuit of justice, has lived a life far richer and more nuanced than the tough-guy exterior he often portrays. Behind the bravado and the brash persona lies a man deeply affected by his experiences, a man grappling with faith, regrets, and a complex sense of triumph.

Dog's faith has been a constant undercurrent throughout his life. Raised in a Southern Baptist household, religion offered him a moral compass during his turbulent youth. Even during his time in prison, faith provided solace and a glimmer of hope for a future beyond bars. However, his journey with faith hasn't been without its detours. The complexities of life, the challenges of his profession, and the personal tragedies he has endured have all tested his beliefs.

One of Dog's most profound regrets stems from his early choices. His involvement in a drug deal gone wrong that resulted in a man's death continues to weigh heavily on him. The guilt and remorse associated with that incident serve as a constant reminder of the devastating consequences of poor decisions. It is a regret that fuels his relentless pursuit of justice, a way, perhaps, to atone for the past by ensuring others don't suffer similar fates.

Yet, Dog's life is not solely defined by regrets. He takes pride in his transformation from a troubled youth to a man dedicated to upholding the law, albeit in his own unconventional way. He sees his work as a bounty hunter as a form of delivering justice, of ensuring that those who break the law are held accountable. The countless fugitives he has apprehended represent, in his mind, a series of triumphs, a testament to his unwavering commitment to a personal code of right and wrong.

Duane 'Dog' Chapman

The loss of his beloved wife, Beth, in 2019, delivered perhaps the most significant blow to Dog's emotional core. Their partnership transcended the professional realm; Beth was his rock, his confidante, and the voice of reason amidst the chaos. Her absence has left a void that no amount of success or bravado can fill. It has forced him to confront his own mortality and re-evaluate his priorities.

Dog Chapman, in his own unfiltered way, grapples with the complexities of life. He is a man of faith tested by hardship, burdened by regret, and driven by a personal sense of justice. The triumphs he celebrates are often unconventional, a reflection of his unorthodox approach to life. However, beneath the tough-guy exterior lies a man capable of introspection, a man forever marked by his experiences, and a man seeking solace and purpose in a world that continues to challenge him.

THE FUTURE OF THE BOUNTY HUNTER

As the sun starts to set on Duane "Dog" Chapman's storied career as a bounty hunter, the question arises: what does the future hold, both for him and for the industry of bounty hunting itself? While his legacy is assured, the landscape of his chosen profession is undergoing a fundamental shift, leaving Dog poised between a revered past and an uncertain future.

Despite his advanced age and recent personal setbacks, Dog remains a restless spirit. He continues to embark on new adventures seeking fugitives and bringing them before the law. Ongoing projects, both televised and independent, keep him in the spotlight, showcasing a passion that refuses to dim. His recent capture of a high-profile suspect in 2023 serves as proof that Dog hasn't lost his touch, a testament to his enduring skills and his relentless drive. However, these pursuits are increasingly shaped by the changing tides of the bounty hunting industry.

The world of bounty hunting is evolving rapidly. Legal restrictions, fueled by controversies surrounding excesses and abuses, are on the rise. Many states have tightened regulations on bail bondsmen and bounty hunters, placing limits on their authority and narrowing their operational capabilities. The rise of technologies like GPS tracking and sophisticated surveillance tools also diminish the need for the traditional bounty hunter's reliance on grit and street smarts.

Furthermore, the public perception of bounty hunting has been tainted by scandals and excesses of the profession. Reality television, while it served to catapult Dog to international fame, also shed light on questionable practices and blurred the lines between entertainment and reality. This evolving public perception, coupled with increasing legal restrictions, poses significant challenges for bounty hunters operating in the mold of Dog Chapman.

However, despite these challenges, it's premature to count Dog Chapman out. He remains a symbol of an era of bounty hunting marked by individualism, unfiltered grit, and a relentless pursuit of justice, even it meant operating on the fringes of the law. His impact on the industry is undeniable; he brought visibility to a profession shrouded in shadows and sparked crucial conversations about its role within the larger justice system.

Duane Chapman's lasting mark on the world of bounty hunting will be one of complexity. He will be remembered as a pioneer, a man who helped shape the public image of the modern-day bounty hunter. However, he will also be seen as a figure representing an era that is gradually fading, replaced by more regulated and technologically-driven approaches. Whether he can adapt to this evolving landscape is a question open for debate.

As for the future of bounty hunting itself, it is one of ongoing transformation. The public's demand for justice remains strong, but the desire for accountability and ethical practices is equally insistent. Bounty hunters who embrace technology, adhere to strict regulations, and operate with transparency and professionalism will chart the path forward. The era of the wild, audacious pursuits embodied by Duane Chapman may be giving way to a more measured and structured approach.

Duane "Dog" Chapman's place in this evolving landscape remains uncertain. His legacy, however, is secure. Love him or hate him, he will forever be remembered as a legendary figure who dared to operate on his own terms, pushing boundaries, provoking controversies, and ultimately shaping our very understanding of what it means to be a bounty hunter.

Made in United States
Troutdale, OR
04/21/2024

19336973R00037